Parenting teenagers is a unique and transfc challenges and rewards. The "Parentinc companion on this journey, offering practical exercises, reflections, and activities designed to help you connect with your teenager, understand their world, and foster a positive and supportive relationship.

Inside this workbook, you will find:

-   Daily Reflections: Guided prompts to help you reflect on your emotions, set goals, and celebrate successes in your parenting journey.

-   Parent-Teen Bonding Activities: Creative ideas and conversation starters to strengthen your relationship and create lasting memories.

-   Self-Care Strategies: Tips and exercises to ensure you are taking care of your own well-being, recognizing that a healthy parent is key to a healthy relationship.

-   Gratitude and Positivity Sections: Spaces to acknowledge the positive aspects of your parenting experience and the unique qualities of your teenager.

-   Improvement Plans: Tools to help you identify areas for growth and make adjustments for a better tomorrow.

-   Connection Strategies: Practical advice for building a deeper connection with your teenager, from active listening to shared interests and beyond.

Whether you are struggling to connect with your teenager or looking for ways to enhance your existing relationship, this workbook is filled with actionable insights and supportive guidance. Each section is crafted to help you navigate the complexities of parenting with patience, understanding, and love.

Embrace the journey of parenting with confidence and compassion. The Parenting Teenagers Workbook is here to support you every step of the way.

Discover, connect, and grow together.

Table of Contents

The Journey Begins 1
Introduction 2
Chapter 1: Understanding Teenagers in 2024 3
Section 1: Self-Reflection 5
Section 2: Parent Teen Bonding 28
Section 3: Self-Care for Parents 51
Section 4: Gratitude and Positivity 58
Section 5: Looking Ahead 65
Connection Strategies 69
Note to Self 71

The Journey Begins

Introduction

Welcome to the Parenting Teenagers Workbook!

Parenting teenagers can be a challenging yet rewarding experience. This workbook is designed to help you connect with your teenager, understand their world, and foster a positive and supportive relationship. Each section includes exercises, reflections, and activities to guide you on this journey.

Chapter 1: Understanding Teenagers in 2024

Parenting a teenager in 2024 comes with its own set of unique challenges and opportunities. This pivotal stage in a young person's life is marked by rapid physical, emotional, and cognitive changes, all against the backdrop of an increasingly digital and interconnected world. As parents, understanding these dynamics is crucial to fostering healthy relationships and guiding our teenagers towards adulthood.

The Modern Teenager

Today's teenagers are growing up in a world vastly different from that of previous generations. They are digital natives, fluent in technology and social media, which shapes much of their social interactions and worldview. This digital landscape offers immense opportunities for learning and connection but also introduces new risks and pressures.

Moreover, societal norms and expectations around gender, identity, and diversity have evolved significantly. Parents navigating these changes must be open-minded, empathetic, and willing to engage in on-going conversations with their teens.

Developmental Milestones

Physiologically, teenagers in 2024 undergo significant changes as their bodies mature. This period is characterized by puberty, hormonal fluctuations, and growth spurts, all of which can influence their behavior and emotional state. Understanding these biological processes helps parents support their teens through what can be a tumultuous time.

Cognitively, teenagers are developing more advanced reasoning skills and beginning to form their own identities separate from their families. They are exploring their values, beliefs, and aspirations, often seeking autonomy while still needing guidance and boundaries from their parents.

Emotional Rollercoaster

Emotionally, teenagers experience a wide range of feelings, from excitement and enthusiasm to insecurity and self-doubt. They may struggle with managing stress, peer pressure, and academic expectations. As parents, providing a safe and supportive environment where teens feel understood and valued is crucial for their emotional well-being.

Parenting Strategies

Navigating the complexities of parenting a teenager in 2024 requires a thoughtful approach. Effective communication, active listening, and setting clear expectations are essential tools for building trust and maintaining positive relationships. Flexibility and

Adaptability is also key as parents respond to the evolving needs and interests of their teens.

Conclusion

Parenting teenagers in 2024 is both challenging and rewarding. By understanding the unique developmental, emotional, and societal factors shaping their lives, parents can better support their teens on their journey to adulthood. This book aims to provide practical insights, strategies, and encouragement to help parents navigate this transformative stage with confidence and compassion.

In the chapters that follow, we will delve deeper into specific aspects of parenting teenagers in 2024, offering guidance on communication, discipline, fostering independence, and nurturing resilience. Together, let's empower ourselves to nurture strong, healthy relationships with our teenagers and prepare them for the opportunities and challenges that lie ahead

Section 1: Self-Reflection

Morning Reflection

How am I feeling today?

(Describe your emotions, any anxieties, or excitements you have about parenting today.)

Day 1.

_____

_____

_____

_____

Day 2.

_____

_____

_____

_____

Day 3.

_____

_____

_____

_____

Day 4.

_____

_____

_____

_____

Day 5.

_____

_____

_____

_____

Day 6.

_____

_____

_____

_____

Day 7.

_____

_____

_____

_____

What are my goals for today?

(Outline any specific goals related to your teenager, such as having a meaningful conversation, supporting them in an activity, or addressing a concern.)

Day 1.

_____

_____

_____

_____

Day 2.

_____

_____

_____

_____

Day 3.

_____

_____

_____

_____

Day 4.

_____

_____

_____

_____

Day 5.

_____

_____

_____

_____

Day 6.

_____

_____

_____

_____

Day 7.

_____

_____

_____

_____

Positive Affirmation for the Day:

"I am patient and understanding."

_____

_____

_____

_____

"I am a loving and supportive parent."

_____

_____

_____

_____

"I am doing my best, and that is enough."

_____

_____

_____

_____

Midday Check-In

What has gone well so far today?

(Note any positive interactions, achievements, or moments of connection with your teenager.)

Day 1.

_____

_____

_____

_____

Day 2.

_____

_____

_____

_____

Day 3.

_____

_____

_____

_____

Day 4.

_____

_____

_____

_____

Day 5.

_____

_____

_____

_____

Day 6.

_____

_____

_____

_____

Day 7.

_____

_____

_____

_____

What challenges have I faced?

(Describe any difficulties or conflicts that have arisen and your response to them.)

Day 1.

_____

_____

_____

_____

Day 2.

_____

_____

_____

_____

Day 3.

_____

_____

_____

_____

Day 4.

_____

_____

_____

_____

Day 5.

_____

_____

_____

_____

Day 6.

_____

_____

_____

_____

Day 7.

_____

_____

_____

_____

How am I managing my stress and emotions?

(Reflect on how you are coping with the day's events and any strategies you are using to stay calm and positive.)

Day 1.

_____

_____

_____

_____

Day 2.

_____

_____

_____

_____

Day 3.

_____

_____

_____

_____

Day 4.

_____

_____

_____

_____

Day 5.

_____

_____

_____

_____

Day 6.

_____

_____

_____

_____

Day 7.

_____

_____

_____

_____

Positive affirmation for the afternoon:

"I handle challenges with grace and patience."

_____
_____
_____
_____

"Every moment is an opportunity to connect with my teenager."

_____
_____
_____
_____

"I am resilient and capable."

_____
_____
_____
_____

Evening Reflection

Highlights of the day:

(Recall and describe any special moments, achievements, or breakthroughs with your teenager.)

Day 1.

_____

_____

_____

_____

Day 2.

_____

_____

_____

_____

Day 3.

_____

_____

_____

_____

Day 4.

_____

_____

_____

_____

Day 5.

_____

_____

_____

_____

Day 6.

_____

_____

_____

_____

Day 7.

_____

_____

_____

_____

What could have gone better?

(Think about any interactions or situations that didn't go as planned and consider what you could do differently next time.)

Day 1.

_____

_____

_____

_____

Day 2.

_____

_____

_____

_____

Day 3.

_____

_____

_____

_____

Day 4.

_____

_____

_____

_____

Day 5.

_____

_____

_____

_____

Day 6.

_____

_____

_____

_____

Day 7.

_____

_____

_____

_____

Section 2: Parent Teen Bonding

How did I support my teenager today?

(List the ways you were there for your teenager, offering emotional support, practical help, or just being present.)

Day 1.

___

___

___

___

Day 2.

___

___

___

___

Day 3.

_____

_____

_____

_____

Day 4.

_____

_____

_____

_____

Day 5.

_____

_____

_____

_____

Day 6.

_____

_____

_____

_____

Day 7.

_____

_____

_____

_____

Positive affirmation for the evening:

"I am grateful for the connection I have with my teenager."

_____

_____

_____

"I learn and grow with each parenting experience."

_____

_____

_____

"I am proud of my efforts and my teenager's progress."

_____

_____

_____

Activity Planning

Activity ideas for tomorrow:

(Plan one or two activities you can do with your teenager to strengthen your bond, such as a shared hobby, a meal together, or a walk.)

Day 1.

_____

_____

_____

_____

Day 2.

_____

_____

_____

Day 3.

_____

_____

_____

_____

Day 4.

_____

_____

_____

_____

Day 5.

_____

_____

_____

_____

Day 6.

_____

_____

_____

_____

Day 7.

_____

_____

_____

_____

Conversation starter:

(Write down an open-ended question or topic to discuss with your teenager to encourage deeper conversation.)

Day 1.

_____

_____

_____

_____

Day 2.

_____

_____

_____

_____

Day 3.

_____

_____

_____

_____

Day 4.

_____

_____

_____

_____

Day 5.

_____

_____

_____

_____

Day 6.

_____

_____

_____

Day 7.

_____

_____

_____

Positive affirmation for bonding:

"I cherish the time spent with my teenager."

_____
_____
_____
_____

"We are building a strong and lasting relationship."

_____
_____
_____
_____

"Our bond grows stronger with each shared moment."

_____
_____
_____
_____

Activity Log

Date: _____ /_____ /_____

Activity:
(Describe the activity you did together.)

Day 1.

_____

_____

_____

_____

Day 2.

_____

_____

_____

Day 3.

_____

_____

_____

_____

Day 4.

_____

_____

_____

_____

Day 5.

_____

_____

_____

_____

Day 6.

_____

_____

_____

_____

Day 7.

_____

_____

_____

_____

What went well?

(Reflect on the positive aspects of the activity.)

Day 1.

_____

_____

_____

_____

Day 2.

_____

_____

_____

_____

Day 3.

_____

_____

_____

_____

Day 4.

_____

_____

_____

_____

Day 5.

_____

_____

_____

_____

Day 6.

_____

_____

_____

_____

Day 7.

_____

_____

_____

_____

What could have gone better?

(Identify any areas for improvement.)

Day 1.

_____

_____

_____

_____

Day 2.

_____

_____

_____

Day 3.

_____

_____

_____

_____

Day 4.

_____

_____

_____

_____

Day 5.

_____

_____

_____

_____

Day 6.

_____

_____

_____

_____

Day 7.

_____

_____

_____

_____

What did I learn about my teenager?

(Note any new insights into their thoughts, feelings, or behaviors.)

Day 1.

_____

_____

_____

_____

Day 2.

_____

_____

_____

_____

Day 3.

_____

_____

_____

_____

Day 4.

_____

_____

_____

_____

Day 5.

_____

_____

_____

_____

Day 6.

_____

_____

_____

_____

Day 7.

_____

_____

_____

_____

Section 3: Self-Care for Parents

Self-Care Checklist

Did I take time for myself today?
(Check off activities you did for your own well-being, such as exercising, reading, meditating, or spending time with friends.)

Day 1.

_____

_____

_____

_____

Day 2.

_____

_____

_____

_____

Day 3.

_____

_____

_____

_____

Day 4.

_____

_____

_____

_____

Day 5.

_____

_____

_____

_____

Day 6.

_____

_____

_____

_____

Day 7.

_____

_____

_____

_____

Self-care plan for tomorrow:

(Identify one or two self-care activities you will prioritize the next day to ensure you are taking care of your own needs.)

Day 1.

_____

_____

_____

Day 2.

_____

_____

_____

Day 3.

_____

_____

_____

_____

Day 4.

_____

_____

_____

_____

Day 5.

_____

_____

_____

_____

Day 6.

_____

_____

_____

_____

Day 7.

_____

_____

_____

_____

Positive affirmation for self-care:

"I deserve time for myself."

_____
_____
_____

"Caring for myself makes me a better parent."

_____
_____
_____

"I am worth the effort of self-care."

_____
_____
_____

Section 4: Gratitude and Positivity

Gratitude Section

Three things I am grateful for today:

Day 1.

_____

_____

_____

_____

Day 2.

_____

_____

_____

_____

Day 3.

_____

_____

_____

_____

Day 4.

_____

_____

_____

_____

Day 5.

_____

_____

_____

_____

Day 6.

_____

_____

_____

_____

Day 7.

_____

_____

_____

_____

One thing I appreciate about my teenager:

(Reflect on a quality or action of your teenager that you are particularly thankful for.)

Day 1.

_____

_____

_____

Day 2.

_____

_____

_____

Day 3.

_____

_____

_____

_____

Day 4.

_____

_____

_____

_____

Day 5.

_____

_____

_____

_____

Day 6.

_____

_____

_____

_____

Day 7.

_____

_____

_____

_____

Positive affirmation for gratitude:

"I am thankful for the joy my teenager brings."

_____

_____

_____

_____

"Gratitude fills my heart and mind."

_____

_____

_____

"I appreciate the journey of parenting."

_____

_____

_____

_____

Section 5: Looking Ahead

What can I do to improve tomorrow?

(Identify any changes or adjustments you can make to enhance your parenting experience and your relationship with your teenager.

Day 1.

_____

_____

_____

Day 2.

_____

_____

_____

Day 3.

_____

_____

_____

_____

Day 4.

_____

_____

_____

_____

Day 5.

_____

_____

_____

_____

Day 6.

_____

_____

_____

_____

Day 7.

_____

_____

_____

_____

Positive affirmation for tomorrow:

"Tomorrow is a new day full of opportunities."

_____

_____

_____

_____

"I am equipped to handle whatever comes my way."

_____

_____

_____

_____

"I look forward to the growth and connection ahead."

_____

_____

_____

_____

Connection Strategies

Ideas for Connecting with Your Teenager

- **Active Listening:** Show genuine interest in what your teenager is saying. Listen more than you speak, and avoid interrupting. Validate their feelings by acknowledging their emotions and experiences.
- **Shared Interests:** Find common ground by identifying activities you both enjoy. This could be anything from watching movies, playing sports, gaming, or even cooking together.
- **Regular One-on-One Time:** Schedule regular one-on-one time with your teenager. This can be as simple as a weekly coffee date, a walk, or any activity that provides an opportunity to connect without distractions.
- **Open-Ended Questions:** Ask open-ended questions that encourage more than yes or no answers. For example, "What was the best part of your day?" or "What do you think about...?"
- **Respect Their Space:** Understand that teenagers need their own space and time. Respect their privacy and encourage independence.
- **Be Supportive, Not Judgemental:** Offer support and understanding instead of judgment. Show empathy and avoid criticism, which can create distance.
- **Participate in Their World:** Show interest in your teenager's hobbies, music, and favorite shows or games. Even if you don't understand or like them, being involved can create a sense of connection.
- **Family Rituals:** Establish family traditions or rituals. Whether it's a weekly game night, movie night, or Sunday dinner, these routines can provide consistent opportunities for bonding.
- **Encourage Expression:** Encourage your teenager to express themselves, whether through art, writing, music, or another outlet. Show appreciation for their efforts and creations.
- **Be Available:** Make sure your teenager knows you are there for them. Sometimes just being present is enough. Let them know they can come to you with anything.
- **Positive Reinforcement:** Focus on positive reinforcement rather than punishment. Praise their achievements and efforts, no matter how small.

- **Empathy and Understanding:** Try to understand things from their perspective. Remember what it was like to be a teenager and acknowledge the unique challenges they face today.
- **Joint Projects:** Work on a project together, such as gardening, building something, or even redecorating a room. Working towards a common goal can foster cooperation and connection.
- **Digital Connection:** Embrace technology as a means of connection. Engage with them on social media, play online games together, or even text them to show you're thinking about them.
- **Healthy Discussions:** Encourage discussions on various topics, including current events, values, and interests. This not only helps in understanding each other's viewpoints but also in developing critical thinking skills.
- **Therapeutic Support:** If the disconnect feels too significant, consider family therapy. A professional can provide strategies and a neutral space to improve communication and connection.
- **Show Vulnerability:** Share your own experiences, challenges, and feelings. Showing vulnerability can help your teenager see you as more relatable and approachable.
- **Support Their Friendships:** Show interest in their friends and encourage positive social interactions. Understanding their social circle can provide insights into their world.
- **Teach by Example:** Demonstrate the behaviors and values you wish to see in your teenager. Be the role model of the person you hope they become.
- **Apologize When Needed:** If you've made a mistake, acknowledge it and apologize. This shows humility and sets a powerful example of accountability.

Remember: Building a connection with your teenager takes time, patience, and effort. Every small step towards understanding and bonding can make a significant difference in your relationship.

Note to Self

Message to Myself:

(Write a note of encouragement, a reminder of your strengths, or a piece of advice to carry forward.)

_____

_____

_____

_____

_____

_____

_____

_____

_____

_____

_____

Message to Myself:

Message to Myself:

Message to Myself:

Message to Myself:

Message to Myself:

Dear Parents,

Thank you for taking the time to invest in your relationship with your teenager through this workbook. Parenting during the teenage years can be a complex and often challenging journey, but it's also a time of incredible growth, discovery, and connections.

Throughout this workbook, I have aimed to provide you with practical tools and insights to help you navigate this unique stage of your parenting journey. Each reflection, activity, and affirmation is designed to support you in building a stronger, more meaningful relationship with your teenager.

As you continue to work through these pages , remember that every small step you take towards understanding patience , and connection is a significant one. There will be ups and downs, moments of joy and frustration, but through it all, your dedication and love make all the difference.

Please know that you are not alone. Many parents share your experience and emotions. Reach out to your community, friends or support groups when you need encouragement or advice. Parenting is not a solitary endeavour it thrives on shared Wisdom and support.

Your efforts to connect with your teenager, to listen, and to be present, are invaluable. You are shaping a foundation of trust and love that will endure long beyond these teenage years.

Thank you for allowing me to be a part of your parenting journey. I hope this workbook has been a helpful and encouraging resource for you. Keep moving forward with confidence and compassion, knowing that your role as a parent is truly extraordinary.

With heartfelt appreciation,

Dr. Wilhelmenia C. Williams

Made in the USA
Columbia, SC
07 July 2024